BERNARD FALLON'S LIVERPOOL
Photographs 1967-1974

Five kids, Scotland Road

Foreword

I met Bernard when he became a student of Graphic Design at Liverpool College of Art, where I was Lecturer in Photography. He took to photography and became a regular in the studios and darkroom of Myrtle Street.

Liverpool was a lively place. John Lennon had recently been asked to leave "Graphics", as he was always nodding off at his desk, due to him spending the night playing with the Beatles. One of my colleagues, Bruce Sabine, told Lennon "If you want to make a success of your life, you should pack in that guitar and get down to some work".

My wife Ina and I lived in Percy Street. Nearby lived Sam Walsh, Don McKinley Adrian Henri and Roger McGough. Stuart Sutcliffe was our next-door neighbour and knocked on our door to borrow a sweeping brush, when he knew his Mum was coming to visit. Beryl Bainbridge lived 'round the corner, Fritz Spiegl lived a couple of doors away and there were many more. The whole place buzzed.

Bernard's brother Andrew, who became a very successful designer in Holland, preceded him. After a BA (Hons) degree, Bernard went to Leicester to do a course in proper photography.

Keeping track of what became of students once they graduated was always a bit hit and miss. We'd get reports that so and so had joined such and such design group. One year another designed the Christmas stamps for the Post Office, one became a maker of rocking horses, and yet another had been shot by a nutter outside the Dakota Building in New York.

I heard news of Bernard through his family in Crosby. He made a steady progression through many enviable jobs and eventually moved to California, where he worked as a Stills Photographer in the TV studios. He was assigned to shoot a photo story on fellow Brit Cary Grant and ended up becoming Grant's favourite photographer of choice.

Bernard takes his place in the pantheon of talented Scousers. In my field, the most famous name is undoubtedly Chambré Hardman a classical portraitist who had a house/studio in Rodney Street. In the 70's my wife and I were looking for a house and we saw Chambré, with a view to purchase. We could have afforded the asking price, but when we asked about the Rates, we were told that he paid £1,500.00 a year, which changed our minds about buying 59 Rodney Street. We later realised that he was paying commercial rates and we would have paid domestic rates; considerably less. Thus, my wife and I saved what is now a National Trust museum for the nation.

Chambré worked slowly and very carefully, setting up the camera on a tripod and considering every aspect of the shot. Bernard's work is also considered and carefully planned, but controlled in a different way. Working with a hand-held camera he often gets to know the subject personally, gaining their confidence, then shooting at the crucial moment.

It is knowing that crucial moment that makes the difference in photography. Not all snappers have it; Bernard has it in abundance.

Reg Cox, January 2007

Introduction

"If your pictures aren't good enough, you're not close enough" Robert Capa 1913-1954

I'm in a packed strange pub with a camera getting a few shots of people singing and enjoying themselves. As I look through the viewfinder most are animated and happy. Then I focus on a big man and a woman sitting completely still. They are scowling at me. I feel a chill, turn away and decide to call it a night. As I make my way towards the exit I hear "Hey, you with the camera!" I glance back. There is the big man barging right towards me. "Yes, you" he calls. He comes up to me and points at the camera. "Did you just take a picture of me and me mam with that?" he demands. I step back and apologize for annoying him. "No, of course not, I wouldn't do that, I would never take a picture of you and your mother." He moves unsteadily towards me, "Well, why friggin' not!"

That was St Patrick's Night, 1970, on Scotland Road, Liverpool. I was completing a B.A. in Graphic Design at the Liverpool School of art and specialising in photography. I was taking a lot of photographs to create a photo-essay for my finals. The title was "One Road, 72 pubs" after seeing a letter in the Liverpool Echo that lamented the decline of Scotland Road's community. I counted only 15 pubs left standing. All the others were demolished, along with hundreds of terraced houses and flats. There were acres of lifeless land graphically dissected by paving stones and cobbles where once teeming streets had thrived. Nothing grew and the only green you'd see was on shamrocks and buses. More buildings were falling to feed the new approach roads into the second Mersey Tunnel, the only sign of progress around here in a long time.

Wedding cake, Crosby

Ice cream, Crosby beach

I'd been idly gazing at this dreary scenery over the years from the buses as they trundled through here on the main route between central Liverpool and Great Crosby, where I was born in 1949. My parents Patrick and Catherine had eight children, so our semi-detached house in Princes Avenue was a bit crowded at times. They were both born into large Irish families in County Cork and County Limerick, but had met in Liverpool. My father's dad was a riveter's mate at the Cammell Laird shipyards in Birkenhead. My mother's father was a wheelwright and builder in a little place called Kilfinane.

Growing up in Crosby, my sisters Philomena, Kate and Maria all went to Seafield Convent school, whilst the boys John, Patrick, Paul, Andrew and I headed for St Mary's College, run by the Irish Christian Brothers. Academically, I was pretty useless and most of the time I wanted to leave, except when I was in the physics, art and geography classes. These subjects explained so much about the world around me. All I knew about the future was that someday I would combine some of all this into my life.

Great Crosby was well positioned: we were perched right on the edge of the River Mersey with a huge beach, and we had easy access to the countryside. There were good train and bus services into Liverpool and Southport, which were opposite worlds away.

Sometimes on a Sunday Father would take us out on a "mystery trip" to give Mother a break from children and housework, and for us to see something interesting. We had no idea where we were going until we got there. It might be a walk into Little Crosby and Ince Blundell, where we got to know some of the farmers, or a map-reading trip around Maghull, or a train ride to the Southport fairground.

Mystery trips into Liverpool gave us a great sense of the city's variety, but not its vigour, because it was mostly closed on Sundays. Father might take us on the old Overhead Railway, along, into and around the docks. If it was raining we went to the Museum and the Walker Art Gallery. "Holyrood Chapel by Moonlight" a large picture of the notable Edinburgh ruin, was one of my favourites. Its realism was striking. And no wonder, as I discovered years later. It had been created by a French scenery designer and painter of realistic life called Louis Daguerre who had exhibited his work in Liverpool in the 1820s. He had also spent years trying to invent a good artistic shortcut to making alternative lifelike representations. Eventually he did, in 1839, and it was called photography.

Father's varied visits into Liverpool also took us along the Pier Head, aboard the ferries, up Bidston Hill and into New Brighton with its pier, Martello Tower and where his youngest brother, Father Robert Fallon, was a parish priest.

On Sunday nights, when we were all tucked up in bed, Father would read a couple of brief stories from the Bible, one from the Old Testament and one from the New. Some of these stories were illustrated with strong black and white pen drawings. Then, by popular request, he would spin a tale or two about The Wanderer, his fictional character who solved crimes and defeated evil around Merseyside and other places throughout the mists of time. One Sunday, the Wanderer might be at a mediaeval tournament facing a charging knight, the next week he could be tracking a wartime spy on the Dock Road. The improvised stories also drew upon his experiences as a customs officer inspecting breweries, distilleries and bonded warehouses. From boarding dozens of ships in the Mersey, he had further tales of hidden contraband and forged papers, stowaways and murder: our imaginations were taken on searches down propeller shafts, through engine rooms and into the holds and bilges of old ships.

Mother loved stories as well, and recounted tales of Irish village life and death, travels and the Troubles. Winter nights brought back their memories of the Liverpool Blitz: air raid sirens, ack-ack, searchlights, bombers and falling shrapnel pinging down the street. They took in a bombed-out family, the Nethercotts, who would only sleep under the stairs, the safest spot in an air raid. One night, with buckets of sand, Father extinguished an incendiary bomb that smashed through next door's roof and burned through the ceiling onto the bed below. He recalled lakes of broken glass covering the streets in Bootle, Seaforth and Waterloo as he cycled back from night duty on the Docks and the anguished vicar whose church roof slates had been completely shaken off by the percussion of anti-aircraft guns parked too close.

At the end of the War in Europe my parents 'adopted' a couple of German prisoners from Fort Crosby prisoner-of-war camp, near Hightown. It was part of a government programme to rehabilitate prisoners and prepare them for repatriation. During the week they worked as farm labourers. On Sundays they would visit our house in their worn out Wehrmacht uniforms to have as good an afternoon tea as the Rations permitted. They brought toys carved from scraps of wood and listened to Father's attempts to speak guide-book German. About 20 years later, my brother Paul was in Cologne and paid a visit to one of them. He too, enjoyed a very civil meal. At the end of it, the old soldier produced a photograph of Paul in nappies, sitting on the uniformed German's knee in our front garden in 1946. I often wondered where did that camera come from? Typical of the era, perhaps that cameras were put away and only appeared on auspicious occasions with a film that lasted months, with Easter at one end and Christmas at the other.

Besides religious pictures and family reminiscences, there were other influences in those formative years. One was the delight of going into "town" on the upstairs front seats of the red Ribble double-deckers. As we made the slow airborne glide towards the Lime Street bus station, we gazed into people's lives below. Around Litherland there was evident bomb damage and lots of pre-fabricated temporary homes still standing, years after the war was finished. Of endless interest, too, were the bombed dissections of houses and tenements where you could see pre-war wallpaper surrounding the ancient fireplaces repeated three floors up. Clearly framed memorials of air rage from the 1940's. The damage worsened as the bus went along Stanley Road and passed into Scotland Road. Along this 3/4 of a mile there were huge gaps where terraced back-to-backs once marched up Everton Brow. The area was literally flattened - the city had demolished many homes and removed the residents miles away to new estates in Kirkby, Skelmersdale and Speke. The area looked a mess, and to quote the locals, "What the Luftwaffe failed to do, the city corporation finished off."

Andrew and Paul, my older brothers, were dabbling in photography. They would create Goonish scenes and photograph them. They tried printing negatives with the enlarger and its attendant trays of liquids all on a bed in a darkened bedroom. That was a doomed arrangement from the start. However, things improved when Andrew started at the Liverpool School of Art and discovered a real darkroom. He also started priming me to apply there as well, and I began to assemble a portfolio of drawings and paintings.

Probably the cramped quarters at home developed the family bug for travelling, and we all thrived on chance meetings and tales from strange places, especially those who enjoyed the economy and unpredictability of hitchhiking. I made some conventional school trips to Lourdes and London with a borrowed Kodak foldout camera, but the results were disappointing. The photos from a summer hitchhiking trip in 1965 up the spectacular coast road of Norway into the Arctic Circle seemed to bear little relationship to the experience. They had weak visual interest and no storytelling appeal.

Later, outside our house I photographed an impromptu stunt organised by big brother John. He drove his Vespa piled up with about 6 extra kids and teenagers from the road and tried to see how many more the poor old scooter could carry. His findings may have had something to do with his later university doctorate on the behaviour of wet steam droplets

Tug ropes, Lamey tug on the Mersey

Beach bystanders, Crosby

through turbine blades. As the heavily overloaded scooter spluttered by, I photographed each pass with my new Brownie camera. Eventually the police appeared and we all scarpered. Don't know what John's professors thought, but the photos were great and the act of lunacy was caught on film. Now I had a new objective with people, shoot the essential moment and compose the picture really well.

Another idea was photographing random arrangements of physical interest and one of the best places was on Crosby Beach. In its pre-Gormley days it was littered with hundreds of wartime concrete pyramids and blocks with rusting steel and wire planted to keep out the invading Hun. There were also the tide lines littered with the rubbish chucked overboard from visiting vessels and other unspeakable objects. But it was photogenic junk with ruined lifebelts, foreign fruit crates and bottles, nets, ends of rope, bits of tyres and plastic things all mixed up with flies, seaweed, jellyfish, shells and great globs of oil.

During the summer before I started at the Art School I bought a 35mm camera. It was small and easy to use and I took it on a hitchhiking trip through Europe and Istanbul to Jerusalem. The results were good and many pictures with ordinary people, posed or otherwise, seemed to capture the essence of their environment so long as I connected with them personally and filled the viewfinder.

Lots of dynamic photo-reportage by Don McCullin, Philip Jones-Griffiths, David Hurn and other photographers was being published in the new colour supplements of the national newspapers such as The Daily Telegraph, Sunday Times and the Observer. Whatever I was doing was confirmed or encouraged by the masters of candid photography, especially at the Magnum photo agency, of whom Henri Cartier-Bresson seemed to be the most astute.

On the Art School Foundation Course the tutors were intent on changing our whole attitude and approach to the visual world and constantly challenged us with their assignments. In charge was the gruff, pugilistic Arthur Ballard who managed a variety of courses (in art history, drawing, design, fashion, liberal studies, painting, photography and three-dimension,) taught by John Baum, Maurice Cockerill, Reg Cox, Adrian Henri, Roger McGough, Robin Ray and Sam Walsh. It was an immersion in a remarkable world with other students who were just as passionate about their art in different ways. We were shown how to develop films and make darkroom prints by Reg Cox in the Myrtle Street Photography department. I began to see further possibilities in making interesting pictures and I looked for more lively things to photograph. A neighbour arranged for me to take some photos during his shift aboard a Lamey tug on the Mersey. The wind and tide all dramatised my pictures of the crew working to get the visiting freighter safely into dock.

The tutors generally encouraged us to relate to the world around us. We were motivated to draw, paint and photograph in the vicinity. The city sloped down to the river with many striking perspectives to enhance its battered features. There were also the quiet places such as the Anglican Cathedral graveyard, the nearby dilapidated Georgian terraces and squares, and the virtually abandoned Albert Dock area.

My tutors also recommended the busier spots – Bold Street, the Pier Head, St John's Market and Paddy's Market, near Scotland Road. I loved the sensation of events and scenes materialising in the viewfinder. To me these were all great places to play the sport of candid camera, but Paddy's Market was the best. Not only were there interesting visitors from foreign ships, but there was Liverpool's own diversity, too, including the elderly shawlies, who were the waning evidence of the area's old Irish roots. Many of the crowd gazed with unposed distraction at busy tables of old tools, shoes, bent nails or other delights. Others were vigorously competing for antiques, trinkets, curtains or clothes. It was one of the great places to photograph the ordinary person caught in the tedium of life.

Adrian Henri asked me and a couple of other students who had cameras, if we wanted to create background slides during his poetry readings with Roger McGough and Brian Patten at the Everyman Theatre. We interpreted their work by altering colour slides with letters, bleach, scratches, cigarette burns and any other iconoclastic effects we could think of. This was the era of Liverpool's innovative music and poetry scene, which the American poet Allen Ginsberg had called the "center of the consciousness of the human universe." He may have been onto something, but in reality, much of Liverpool appeared to be in a state of decline, amid its industrial and docks problems. Gradually I was being drawn into those areas, as well.

I roamed around the docks and kept the camera out of sight until necessary. At one point a gang of dockers was busy unloading a ship with cranes and big nets. Showing the camera to one of them I asked if I could get a few photos. It wasn't a problem, and, in fact, his mates were cheerful and helped out: "Wanna get some snaps from up in that crane, lad? Yer get a nice view, y'know. Yes? Hey Joe, stop the crane, you've gotta visitor coming up!"

One great quality of the camera is its ability to balance the tension between beauty and reality. The oily scum floating in the corner of a dock could also reveal strong shapes and brilliant colours. Around the working docks and much of Liverpool there were many interesting scenes and details to photograph. Outside the Albert Dock there was lots of remarkable sculptured stone to soften the impact on Victorian sailing ships manouvering against a racing tide, entering or leaving the river. When it snowed, Liverpool enjoyed a muffled quietness and a short but lovely facelift. The sooty Victorian brickwork and other architectural details enjoyed a mini revival as the snow highlighted their extraordinary craftsmanship.

Over the next couple of years I looked for photographic interpretations to the art school assignments whenever possible. We were given lots of leeway to specialise in our favoured fields. In my final year I started shooting the Scotland Road project. The photography instructors, Reg Cox and Tudor Williams gave me plenty of guidance with shooting pictures. For instance, in a poorly lit pub how could you move around and shoot without slow shutter problems? I didn't want to use flash: it was very distracting and it also totally changed the room's atmosphere. Another problem was that flash picked up cigarette smoke. The solution was to push the film's capabilities in exposure and in its subsequent development. Once I'd got the hang of this technique, I felt at ease going almost anywhere with the camera. Cox, along with the Design and Illustration instructors Messrs Chidwick, Daffern, Derbyshire, Fields and Sabine were all very fond of Liverpool and helped nudge the project along and critique it where necessary. Ray Fields' frequent exhortations to the students to "use plenty of colour" and "get involved!" rang in my ears.

I started with the obvious scenes of the massive Mersey Tunnel operations at the southern end of Scotland Road. It must have given work to hundreds, but changed the lives of thousands. As one man said, "All this, just to get to Birkenhead?" Around busy streets and people's homes there was a confusing mixture of excavation, demolition and construction. It was usually easy to relate to the labourers and drivers, partly because of my summer jobs on building sites, timber yards and the docks. Mostly though, it was because the working Scouser is very friendly and curious, more than happy to stop and have a chat with someone holding a camera.

A lot of the Catholic and Protestant rivalry was dissipated in the slum clearances, but you could still see large sections of graffiti from each side boldly splashed on walls. I remember talking to Father Smith at St Anthony's Church on Scotty Road. He told me that one evening before midnight two drunks banged on the door and one of them said, "Father, I'm a Catholic and you've got to baptize this man immediately. He's an Orangeman and I've just spent a fortune in the pub tonight, convincing him to switch sides." "Couldn't this wait until tomorrow morning?" asked the priest. "Certainly not,

15

Mr Burke, Waterloo Sweep, Litherland

Two boys, off Scotland Road

Father. When he sobers up, he might change his mind!" Another time an Orangeman told me straightfaced that on his deathbed he was going to call a Catholic priest for absolution and be converted just as he died. I couldn't believe this, so I asked why? "So that when I go, there'll be one less of them!" he replied.

As I took more photographs, I did get more involved and moved closer to people I thought represented the spirit of the moment. On Islington was Regan's Doss House where many indigent Liverpudlians went. The owner gave me his blessing to shoot some pictures, but I handed out cups of tea and cigarettes just to smooth the way and to maintain a cooperative distance with everyone. My method was to never disturb the ambiance, just to record it. If they weren't interested they shook their heads, and I moved away. There was no hostility at all, which is what I had imagined might happen.

On one of the vast wastelands I met a couple of men with a handcart burning piles of clothes. "As it's Corpy land, it's our job to clean it up. We take out the decent stuff like the iron bed, but we have to burn the mattresses, because they are full of disease – like crabs. It's all due to the families moving out. They just chuck the stuff out; all over the place. Tons of it everywhere, and there's only me and Frank there, with the barrow." Their fire had attracted some boys and girls who were now jumping through the smoke. "Hey you kids. Hop it; yer mam wants yer."

On the way home driving past another wasteland in Seaforth I saw a tinkers' encampment and thought it must be difficult to get good photographs there. After all I was the outsider to them, and they probably viewed me with suspicion. The first step obviously was to talk to them and get their acceptance. This turned out to be easy, as another student Steve Jacobson wanted to buy a camping gas cylinder to help airbrush some new paintings. I steered Steve down to the encampment and while he examined cylinders and checked valve fittings, I asked a couple of the older men about taking a few snaps. It worked out very well for all concerned. Everyone got what they wanted and I ended up visiting the tinkers a few more times. The hardest part was trying to keep the kids from constantly crowding into the camera lens. Talk about getting close to the subject! They were just like new puppies jumping up for attention. Eventually, over a couple of visits I was invited into their caravans to sit down, relax have a cuppa and take a photograph or two. They were a lively and funny bunch of people. I wondered how many lived in some of the caravans and thought of my own upbringing, which was nothing like this. Physically, things were different, but on some levels I saw similar stuff. Older kids leading or dominating smaller ones and mothers stuck with domestic duty. And then there was the special occasion of the newborn baby in nappies arranged carefully on the knee. "Would you take its photograph, mister? No one around here seems to have a camera."

I began to like photographing interiors for their quiet statements about the human condition, but around Scotland Road, some of the exteriors were less than eloquent. I photographed a partially roofless block of flats being dismantled that still housed an elderly couple waiting nervously to be evacuated. It could have been a recreation of the Blitz, if the building hadn't been so new. The couple didn't want to leave and go to Kirkby. They'll have to make new friends and he'll have to find a new pub. "You get moved into a new flat with a bath and things. You haven't got no friends. Yer in a box watchin' another box. You'll just fret and die." Scenes of destruction were always depressing in the end, so I'd try to balance it out with something a bit more lively around Scotty Road. Invariably people were amused by my presence, asked a few questions and then got on with their business. The betting shops were friendly places and lots of women seemed to go there during the week. Some of the men grumbled at the ladies' apparent lack of skill, "They spend flaming pounds here, and then they have their bloody bingo. So no wonder the lads go on flippin' strike."

Monday morning in the old public laundry was a great place to be, just don't get in the way of all the busy women. It was steamy, cheap and perfect for processing the weekend's events and gossip in between washing, drying and folding. "I'm telling yer, son," one of them told me, "There's more news going through here than the "Echo." We only read them papers to confirm what we heard last week."

About half of the photographs in this book were taken in the Scotland Road area in 1969 and 1970. After I graduated from the Art School, I travelled through Spain, and completed a post-grad year in photography at Leicester Polytechnic School of Design. This was an introduction to studio cameras, different lighting techniques and processing colour film. Later, I went to Ireland and visited California for six months. After returning to Crosby I started looking at some of the local places and characters who might be worth revisiting. I thought about the train rides into Liverpool over the years. Perhaps the route was less personal than the busses, but the railway workers and signal box crew were interesting and cooperative. Those and a couple of chimney sweeps caught my eye. At Aintree, Red Rum was gaining fame, so I joined the festivities, and like Paddy's Market, at the other end of the A59, it was a great place to go to. There was now a steadier hand and eye behind the camera and I assembled an improving portfolio of photographs.

Now I'm in a huge, dark television studio at the BBC in London. This is my first job with a camera and it's going to last three weeks. I am taking shots of the empty sets of a new period drama with a Leica on a tripod, loaded with Type B tungsten colour slide film. The fake rooms are solid sections of a bygone era in Vienna and are enhanced with realistic props and painted *tromp l'oeil* panels selectively lit by overhead rows of lights. It's a bright and impressive illusion. Louis Daguerre would have loved it. There are no actors and no crew around. It's totally quiet and I take the shots very slowly and deliberately. First do the wide views and then move in for the details. The set designers and construction people like a nice visual record of this temporary world just in case they wish to revisit it. Here I am in a whole new world of colour and far from home.

That was in July 1973. All the photographs taken in Liverpool seemingly had no further purpose any more, so they were packed away in a box. Not pictures of streets and roads and avenues, but moments of a time growing up. To look at them some might see places and others might see faces. They were in fact gestures and reactions, those little fractions of acceptance between strangers and myself. Some a cold moment of the obedient shutter. Others the synchronisation of the human spirit captured in an unspoken contract. The photographs contained an important era for me and I took it with me wherever I lived in London and later in California. On the brief visits back to Merseyside over the next 30 years I thought about the times I had wandered around Liverpool and all the people I had photographed. There were about 90 rolls of film. Maybe I should re-print a couple and see how they look? Perhaps show them somewhere? The little Scouse voice in the box of negatives became a bit louder. "Hey, mister, take me pictures. Yes, take me pictures – take them back home to Liverpool."

I hope you enjoy looking at them as much as I enjoyed taking them.

Curlers, train cleaner, Hall Road

Our alley, back of my house, Crosby

Snowball, Regent Road, Crosby

Above Great Georges Street

Bag of laundry, Scotland Road

Delivery, stone thrower, near Scotland Road

Day off, Crosby beach

Talking, Blackstock Street by the Northern General Hospital

Grannies, Scotland Road

Laundry gossip, off Scotland Road

Purses, Paddy's Market

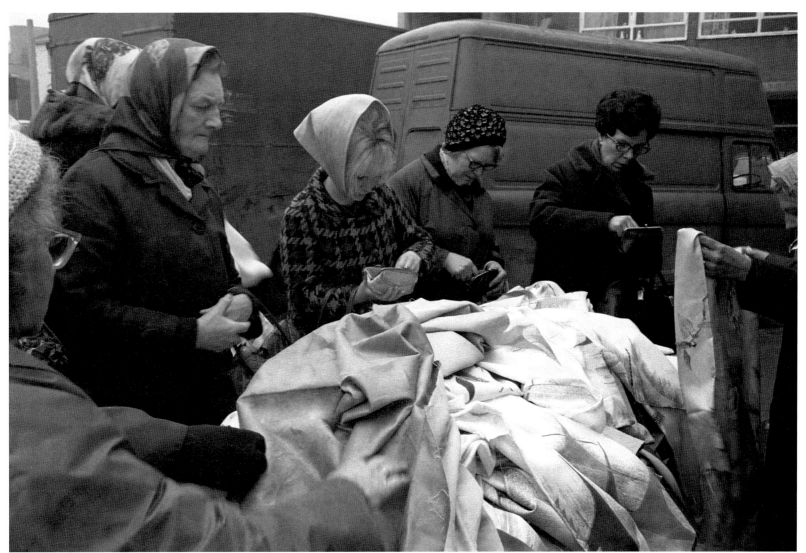

Pets, Paddy's Market

Prams, Crosby

44

The Place, near Everton Brow

Favourites, Scotland Road

Two women, pub, Scotland Road

Opening time, Scotland Road

Shawlie and husband

City sanitation, off Scotland Road

"Make us famous", off Scotland Road

The long walk, Everton Brow

Neighbours, Scotland Road area

Final residents, near Scotland Road

Warehouses, Vauxhall

Second entrance, Kingsway Tunnel, Scotland Road

Steel framers, Kingsway Tunnel, Scotland Road

Shelter soup, Regan's Doss House, Islington

Point taken, Regan's Doss House, Islington

The tinkers' baby, Seaforth

Tinker camp, Seaforth

Stall, Dock Road, Seaforth

Wood

Grain barge

Three tugs

Cigarette

Toilets, strike site at timber yard, Waterloo

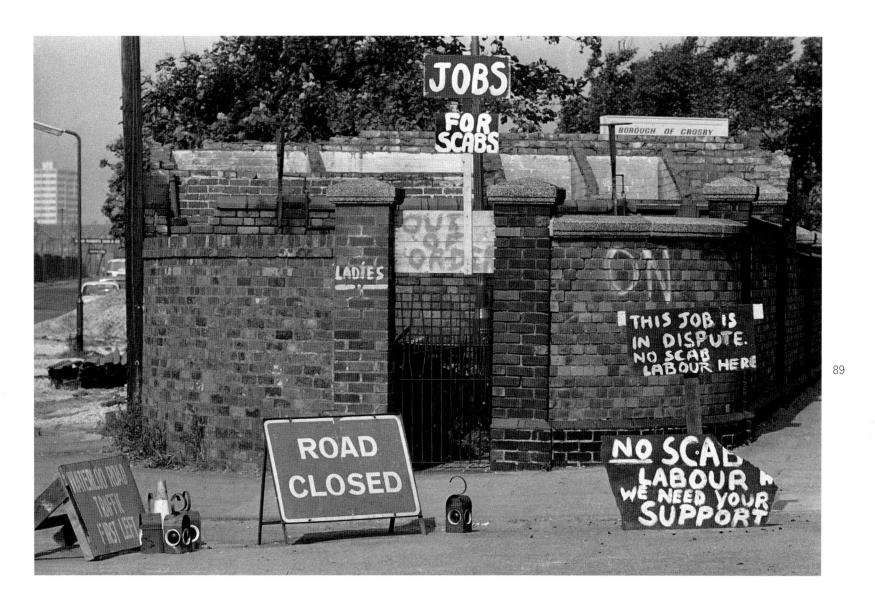

89

T–break, Byrom Street

Wet paint

'God Bless Our Pope'

95

'Vote Protestant'

Orange Lodge parade, Southport

Racegoers, Aintree Grand National

Aintree rollers, Grand National

Beer, Aintree Grand National

JC and Jacey, nativity, Clayton Square

Mustard, Liverpool city centre

Shopping, Church Street

Acknowledgements

My thanks are due to Fiona Philpott, Director of Exhibitions at National Museums Liverpool. Fiona first expressed interest in creating the exhibition upon which this book is based, after seeing a small sample of photographs that I sent her in early 2006. My sister Maria Guidera had helped create this opportunity through contacts at her work with the Liverpool charity PSS.

Paul Gallagher and Annie Lord of NML were my regular weekly links as we started to turn a shortlist of two hundred photographs into a final edition of sixty framed images. Many thanks are due for their professionalism, patience and humour in translating many ideas into a greater vision that the photographs now convey.

The process of creating the archival prints from film negatives and colour slides required hours of retouching the hundreds of spots and scratches that the emulsions had acquired over the years. My sons Patrick and Daniel played a major role in the restoration, printing and production process of all the photographs in this book. Thanks are also due to Stephanie Dansky for her time and effort with retouching many of the images.

My brothers and sisters Andrew, John, Kate, Maria, Patrick, Paul and Philomena all provided valuable assistance in clarifying some of our misty family history. Patrick ran his critical eye over my draft without changing its style. Reg Cox my former photography tutor at the Liverpool School of Art also helped with its historical context and accuracy.

Finally, my parents Catherine and Patrick Fallon CBE should be mentioned with affection: they crossed the Irish Sea and made their unique contribution to this great town that I know so well.

Bernard Fallon, February 2007